FLORIDA

EXPLORE THE UNITED STATES ★ EXPLORE THE UNITED STATES ★ EXPLORE THE UNITED STATES ★ EXPLORE THE UNITED STATES

Sarah Tieck

Big Buddy BOOKS
Explore the United States

VISIT US AT
www.abdopublishing.com

Published by ABDO Publishing Company, PO Box 398166, Minneapolis, MN 55439.

Printed in the United States of America, North Mankato, Minnesota.
032012
092012

♻ PRINTED ON RECYCLED PAPER

Coordinating Series Editor: Rochelle Baltzer
Contributing Editors: Megan M. Gunderson, BreAnn Rumsch, Marcia Zappa
Graphic Design: Adam Craven
Cover Photograph: *Shutterstock*: Jason Patrick Ross.
Interior Photographs/Illustrations: *AP Photo*: AP Photo (p. 23), Vince Bucci/Picture Group via AP IMAGES (p. 23), NASA, HO (p. 19), North Wind Picture Archives via AP Images (p. 13); *Getty Images*: Central Press (p. 25); *Glow Images*: Destinations (p. 27), Superstock (p. 5); *iStockphoto*: ©iStockphoto.com/HelloBrianHogan (p. 19), ©iStockphoto.com/jcarillet (p. 26), ©iStockphoto.com/kjohansen (p. 30), ©iStockphoto.com/Marje (p. 30), ©iStockphoto.com/Paulbr (p. 13), ©iStockphoto.com/THEPALMER (p. 27); *Shutterstock*: Steve Byland (p. 30), Darren K. Fisher (p. 26), Marek Gahura (p. 11), Judy Kennamer (p. 9), Daniel Korzeniewski (p. 17), kurdistan (p. 29), Phillip Lange (p. 30), Eran Meyer (p. 21), Daniel Padavona (p. 19), Henryk Sadura (p. 9), R. Gino Santa Maria (p. 11), Edwin Verin (p. 27).

All population figures taken from the 2010 US census.

Library of Congress Cataloging-in-Publication Data

Tieck, Sarah, 1976-
  Florida / Sarah Tieck.
    p. cm. -- (Explore the United States)
  ISBN 978-1-61783-347-2
  1. Florida--Juvenile literature. I. Title.
  F311.3.T54 2013
  975.9--dc23
                          2012003046

Contents

One Nation

The United States is a **diverse** country. It has farmland, cities, coasts, and mountains. Its people come from many different backgrounds. And, its history covers more than 200 years.

Today, the country includes 50 states. Florida is one of these states. Let's learn more about Florida and its story!

Did You Know?

Florida became a state on March 3, 1845. It was the twenty-seventh state to join the nation.

Florida is home to the Florida Keys. Long bridges connect this island chain to mainland Florida.

FLORIDA UP CLOSE

The United States has four main **regions**. Florida is in the South.

Florida has two states on its borders. Georgia and Alabama are to the north. The Atlantic Ocean is east and south. The Gulf of Mexico is west.

Florida has a total area of 58,976 square miles (152,747 sq km). About 18.8 million people live in the state.

REGIONS OF THE UNITED STATES

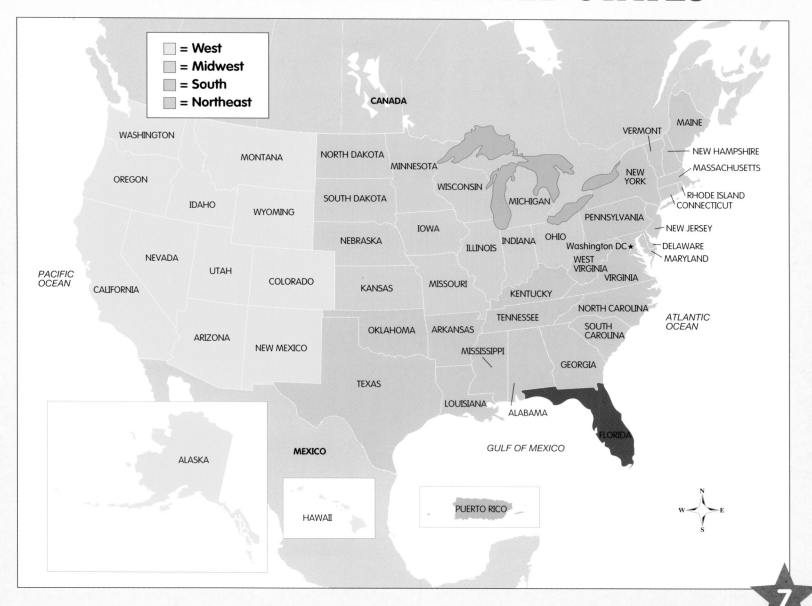

☐	= West
☐	= Midwest
☐	= South
☐	= Northeast

CANADA

WASHINGTON

MONTANA

NORTH DAKOTA

MINNESOTA

VERMONT

MAINE

NEW HAMPSHIRE

OREGON

MASSACHUSETTS

IDAHO

WYOMING

SOUTH DAKOTA

WISCONSIN

MICHIGAN

NEW YORK

RHODE ISLAND
CONNECTICUT

PENNSYLVANIA

NEW JERSEY

NEVADA

UTAH

NEBRASKA

IOWA

ILLINOIS

INDIANA

OHIO

Washington DC ★

DELAWARE
MARYLAND

WEST VIRGINIA

VIRGINIA

PACIFIC OCEAN

CALIFORNIA

COLORADO

KANSAS

MISSOURI

KENTUCKY

NORTH CAROLINA

ATLANTIC OCEAN

ARIZONA

NEW MEXICO

OKLAHOMA

ARKANSAS

TENNESSEE

SOUTH CAROLINA

MISSISSIPPI

GEORGIA

TEXAS

LOUISIANA

ALABAMA

FLORIDA

ALASKA

MEXICO

GULF OF MEXICO

HAWAII

PUERTO RICO

N
W · E
S

IMPORTANT CITIES

Tallahassee is the **capital** of Florida. It is home to 181,376 people. Its name means "old town." And, it has a long history. In 1539, Spanish explorer Hernando de Soto camped near there.

Jacksonville is the state's largest city. Its population is 821,784. It is also one of the biggest US cities in land size. The city covers more than 800 square miles (2,000 sq km)!

Did You Know?

The upper part of Florida is shaped like the handle of a frying pan. So, it is called the "panhandle."

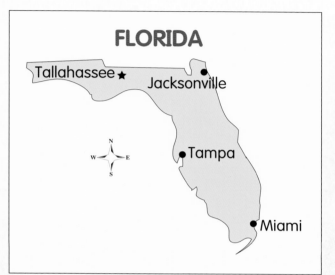

FLORIDA

Tallahassee ★
Jacksonville
Tampa
Miami

N W E S

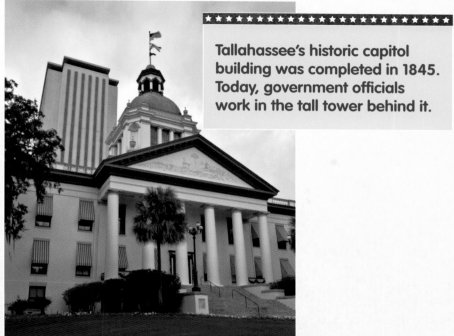

Tallahassee's historic capitol building was completed in 1845. Today, government officials work in the tall tower behind it.

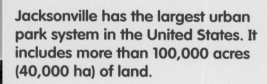

Jacksonville has the largest urban park system in the United States. It includes more than 100,000 acres (40,000 ha) of land.

9

Miami is Florida's second-largest city. It is home to 399,457 people. This city is a popular vacation spot. It is known for its beautiful beaches.

Tampa is the state's third-largest city. Its population is 335,709. Tampa is another popular vacation spot. It is located on Tampa Bay.

★★★★★★★★★★★★★★★★★★★★★★★★★★★
Tall hotels and apartment buildings line Miami's beaches.

★★★★★★★★★★★★★★★★★★★★★★★★★★★★★★★★★★★★★
Tampa has the largest deepwater port in Florida. Many big ships come and go from there.

FLORIDA IN HISTORY

Florida's history includes European explorers and Native Americans. Spanish explorers first arrived in present-day Florida in 1513. Native Americans had already lived there for thousands of years.

In 1565, the Spanish built a settlement in northeastern Florida. It was named Saint Augustine. It is the oldest **permanent** settlement in the United States.

For many years, Spain and England fought over land in Florida. Florida became a US territory in 1822. It became a state in 1845.

Juan Ponce de León led Spanish explorers to Florida in 1513. He was looking for a magical fountain of youth!

Did You Know?

Ponce de León named Florida after *Pascua Florida*, the Spanish name for Easter.

Saint Augustine is home to the oldest stone fort in the United States. Spanish settlers built it in the late 1600s to protect the area.

Timeline

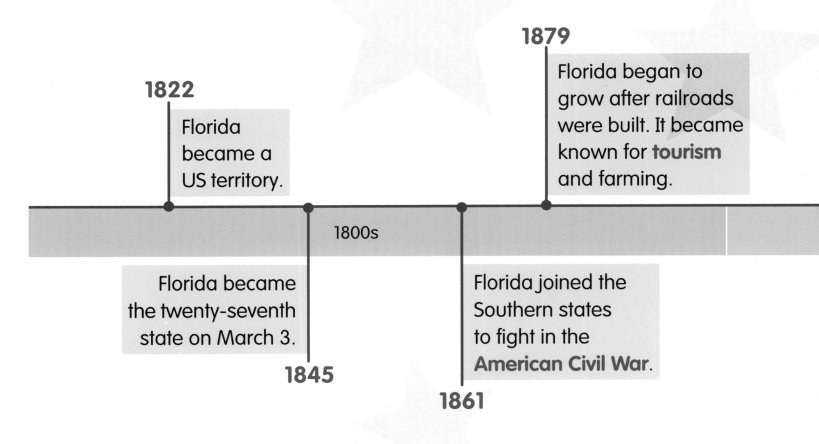

1822

Florida became a US territory.

1845

Florida became the twenty-seventh state on March 3.

1861

Florida joined the Southern states to fight in the **American Civil War**.

1879

Florida began to grow after railroads were built. It became known for **tourism** and farming.

1800s

2010

An oil well broke and about 200 million gallons (760 million L) of oil spilled into the Gulf of Mexico near Pensacola Beach. This was the worst offshore oil spill in US history.

1971

Walt Disney World Resort's Magic Kingdom opened in Orlando.

2003

The Tampa Bay Buccaneers won the Super Bowl!

1900s

2000s

The Miami Dolphins won the Super Bowl! They won again in 1974.

Hurricane Andrew was one of the most destructive storms to ever hit Florida.

Four hurricanes hit Florida within about six weeks.

1973

2004

1992

ACROSS THE LAND

Florida is known for its islands, beaches, and palm trees. The Florida Keys are islands off the state's southern tip. Florida also has **swamps** and flat, open land. Big Cypress Swamp and the Everglades cover much of southern Florida.

Many types of animals make their homes in Florida. These include alligators, herons, and flamingos. Dolphins and manatees swim in the coastal waters.

Did You Know?

Most of Florida is hot and humid in the summer. In Tallahassee, the average July temperature is 83°F (28°C).

The Everglades is thick with plants. It is also home to uncommon animals. These include Florida panthers and American crocodiles.

17

EARNING A LIVING

Transportation, farming, and **tourism** are important businesses in Florida. Goods are shipped through Florida's port cities. Fruits and vegetables are grown in the state. And, many people have jobs helping visitors.

Space programs are also important to business in Florida. John F. Kennedy Space Center is in Cape Canaveral. There, workers plan US space travel.

Did You Know?

Florida's warm weather allows fresh fruit to grow all year. So, Florida supplies fruit to the rest of the United States. This is important to the northern states during the winter.

The last space shuttle took off from Kennedy Space Center in July 2011. Scientists there are working on new kinds of space travel.

Oranges are an important crop in Florida. The state makes almost half the world's orange juice!

19

Sports Page

When many people think of Florida, they think of sports. The state is home to several football, baseball, basketball, and hockey teams. Golf events and car races are held there, too.

College sports are also popular in Florida. Miami hosts the Orange Bowl every year on or near New Year's Day. Two top college football teams play in the Orange Bowl.

Baseball teams from around the country have spring training in Florida. The state's warm weather makes it an ideal place for this.

HOMETOWN HEROES

Many famous people have lived in Florida. Actor Sidney Poitier was born in Miami around 1927. He was the first black actor to win an **Academy Award** for a leading part in a movie. He won for the 1963 movie *Lilies of the Field*.

When Poitier began acting, black people did not have the same rights as other Americans. His work helped make more opportunities for others.

22

Poitier is known for the movies *Lilies of the Field* (*left*) and *Guess Who's Coming to Dinner.*

Poitier continues to be a well-respected actor.

23

Tennessee Williams was a famous writer of plays. He was born in Missouri in 1911. He first visited Key West in 1941. Later, he bought a house there. He lived in Key West off and on for more than 30 years. Williams is known for writing *A Streetcar Named Desire* and *Cat on a Hot Tin Roof*.

Williams was honored with two Pulitzer Prizes for his plays.

Tour Book

Do you want to go to Florida? If you visit the state, here are some places to go and things to do!

 ## Taste

Grab a slice of key lime pie. This is a Florida favorite! Or, try fresh seafood, such as Atlantic white shrimp.

 ## Relax

Visit one of Miami's beaches. You could swim in the ocean, build a sand castle, or look for seashells!

 ## Explore

Take an airboat ride or walk the boardwalks in the Everglades. Maybe you'll see an alligator or a crocodile!

 ## Play

Spend a day at the Magic Kingdom near Orlando. This is one of the world's most-visited theme parks!

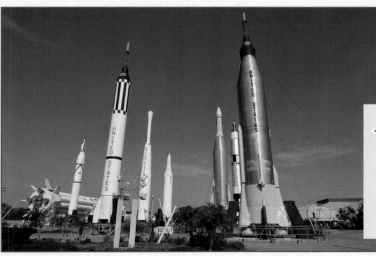

 ## Discover

Visit Kennedy Space Center to learn about space travel. You can see historic rockets in the Rocket Garden!

A Great State

The story of Florida is important to the United States. The people and places that make up this state offer something special to the country. Together with all the states, Florida helps make the United States great.